Jackie Robinson

Baseball Legend

by Grace Hansen

ABDO
HISTORY MAKER BIOGRAPHIES
Kids

abdopublishing.com

Published by Abdo Kids, a division of ABDO, PO Box 398166, Minneapolis, Minnesota 55439.

Copyright © 2015 by Abdo Consulting Group, Inc. International copyrights reserved in all countries. No part of this book may be reproduced in any form without written permission from the publisher.

Printed in the United States of America, North Mankato, Minnesota.

102014

012015

 THIS BOOK CONTAINS RECYCLED MATERIALS

Photo Credits: AP Images, Corbis, Getty Images, iStock, © Michael Rivera / CC-SA-3.0 p.5
Production Contributors: Teddy Borth, Jennie Forsberg, Grace Hansen
Design Contributors: Laura Rask, Dorothy Toth

Library of Congress Control Number: 2014943713

Cataloging-in-Publication Data

Hansen, Grace.

 Jackie Robinson: baseball legend / Grace Hansen.

  p. cm. -- (History maker biographies)

Includes index.

ISBN 978-1-62970-701-3

1. Robinson, Jackie, 1919-1972--Juvenile literature. 2. Baseball players--United States--Biography--Juvenile literature. 3. African American baseball players --Juvenile literature. 1. Title.

796.357092--dc23

[B]

2014943713

Table of Contents

Early Life

Jackie Robinson was born on January 31, 1919. He was born in Cairo, Georgia.

Georgia

WELCOME TO CAIRO GEORGIA'S Hospitality City

5

Jackie was a great athlete. He played baseball and basketball. He played football and track, too.

Jackie went to **UCLA**. He earned **varsity** letters in four sports. He was the first UCLA athlete to do this.

The Kansas City Monarchs

Jackie could no longer afford UCLA. He served in the army for two years. Then he played for the Kansas City Monarchs. It was an all-black baseball team.

11

Family

In 1946, Jackie married Rachel Islum. They had three children.

13

Breaking the Color Barrier

Branch Rickey was the president of the Brooklyn Dodgers. In 1945, he asked Jackie to play for him. Jackie would be the first black man on the team.

15

Jackie played very well his **rookie** year. But, he dealt with **racism**. It was very hard for him.

Dodgers Career

Jackie played baseball for 10 years. He was more than a great ball player. He ended **segregation** in baseball.

Life after Baseball

After baseball, Jackie worked for **social change**. He was also a businessman. He died on October 24, 1972.

Timeline

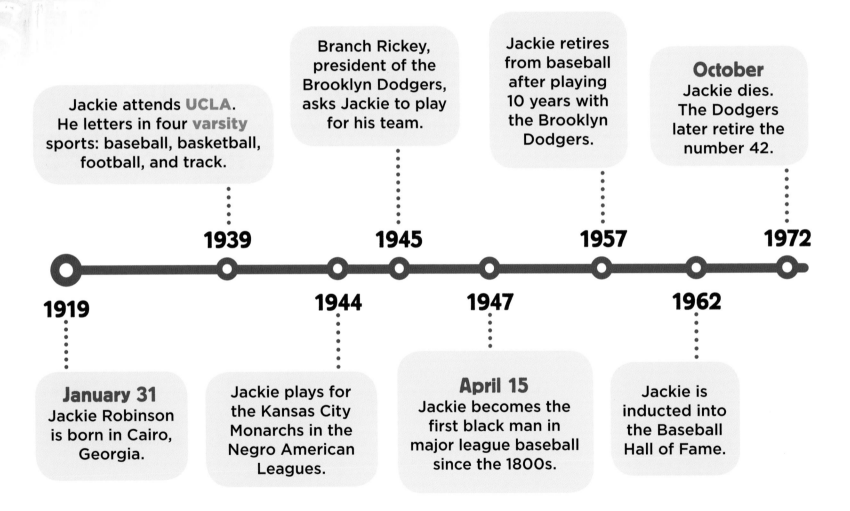

Jackie attends **UCLA**. He letters in four **varsity** sports: baseball, basketball, football, and track.

Branch Rickey, president of the Brooklyn Dodgers, asks Jackie to play for his team.

Jackie retires from baseball after playing 10 years with the Brooklyn Dodgers.

October
Jackie dies. The Dodgers later retire the number 42.

1939   **1945**   **1957**   **1972**

1919   **1944**   **1947**   **1962**

January 31
Jackie Robinson is born in Cairo, Georgia.

Jackie plays for the Kansas City Monarchs in the Negro American Leagues.

April 15
Jackie becomes the first black man in major league baseball since the 1800s.

Jackie is inducted into the Baseball Hall of Fame.

Glossary

racism – treating someone poorly or using violence against them because of the color of their skin.

rookie – a first-year player in a sport.

segregation – the practice of keeping people of different races, religions, etc., separate from each other.

social change – refers to a change in the way things are in society. Jackie Robinson wanted to change the way life was for black people in the United States.

UCLA – short for University of California, Los Angeles.

varsity – the main team at a high school or college in a certain sport. Every player on a varsity team earns a letter. A letter is like an award.

23

Index

abdokids.com

Use this code to log on to abdokids.com and access crafts, games, videos, and more!

Abdo Kids Code:
HJK7013